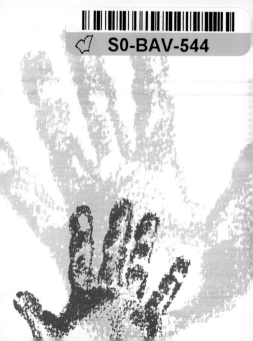

Another Sip of Chicken Soup for the Soul®

Heartwarming Stories of the Love Between Parents and Children

Inspired by the #1 *New York Times* bestseller

Chicken Soup for the Soul®

by Jack Canfield and Mark Victor Hansen

Tommy's Essay

by Jane Lindstrom

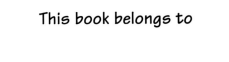

This book belongs to

_____

Another Sip of Chicken Soup for the Soul®

Heartwarming Stories of the Love Between Parents and Children

Andrews McMeel Publishing

Kansas City

ISBN: 0-8362-5088-5

A gray sweater hung limply on Tommy's empty desk, a reminder of the dejected boy who had just followed his classmates from our third-grade room. Soon Tommy's parents, who had recently separated, would arrive for a conference on his failing schoolwork and disruptive behavior. Neither parent knew that I had summoned the other.

Tommy, an only child, had always been happy, cooperative and an excellent student. How could I convince his father and mother that his recent failing grades represented a brokenhearted child's reaction to his adored parents' separation and pending divorce?

Tommy's mother entered and took one of the chairs I had placed near my desk. Soon the father arrived. Good! At least they were concerned enough to be prompt. A look of surprise and irritation passed between them, and then they pointedly ignored each other.

As I gave a detailed account of Tommy's behavior and schoolwork, I prayed for the right words to bring these two together, to help them see what they were doing to their son. But somehow the words wouldn't come. Perhaps if they saw one of his smudged, carelessly done papers.

I found a crumpled, tear-stained sheet stuffed in the back of his desk, an English paper. Writing covered both sides — not the assignment, but a single sentence scribbled over and over.

Silently I smoothed it out and gave it to Tommy's mother. She read it and then without a word handed it to her husband. He frowned. Then his face softened. He studied the scrawled words for what seemed an eternity.

At last he folded the paper carefully, placed it in his pocket and reached for his wife's out-stretched hand. She wiped the tears from her eyes and smiled up at him. My own eyes were brimming, but neither seemed to notice. He helped her with her coat, and they left together.

In his own way God had given me the words to reunite that family. He had guided me to the sheet of yellow copy paper covered with the anguished outpouring of a small boy's troubled heart.

The words, "Dear Mother...Dear Daddy...I love you...I love you...I love you."

Children Learn What They Live

by Dorothy L. Nolte

If children live with criticism,
    they learn to condemn.

If children live with hostility,
    they learn to fight.

If children live with fear,
    they learn to be apprehensive.

If children live with pity,
    they learn to feel sorry for themselves.

If children live with ridicule,
    they learn to be shy.

If children live with jealousy,
    they learn what envy is.

If children live with shame,
    they learn to feel guilty.

If children live with tolerance,
they learn to be patient.

If children live with encouragement,
they learn to be confident.

If children live with praise,
they learn to appreciate.

If children live with approval,
they learn to like themselves.

If children live with acceptance,
they learn to find love in the world.

If children live with recognition,
they learn to have a goal.

If children live with sharing,
they learn to be generous.

If children live with honesty and fairness,
they learn what truth and justice are.

If children live with security,
they learn to have faith in themselves
and in those around them.

If children live with friendliness,
they learn that the world is a nice
place in which to live.

If children live with serenity,
they learn to have peace of mind.

With what are your children living?

I

I Love
You, Son

by Victor B. Miller

Thoughts while driving my son to school: Morning, Kid. You look pretty sharp in your Cub Scout gear, not as fat as your old man when he was a Cub. I don't think my hair was ever as long until I went away to college, but I think I'd recognize you anyway by what you are: a little shaggy around the ears, scuffed around the toes, wrinkled in the knees. ... We get used to one another. ...

Now that you're eight I notice I don't see a whole lot of you anymore. On Columbus Day you left at nine in the morning. I saw you for 42 seconds at lunch, and you reappeared for supper at five. I miss you, but I know you've got serious business to take care of. Certainly as serious as, if not more important than, the things the other commuters on the road are doing.

You've got to grow up and out, and that's more important than clipping coupons, arranging stock options or selling people short. You've got to learn what you are able to do and what you aren't — and you've got to learn how to deal with that. You've got to learn about people and how they behave when they don't feel good about themselves — like the bullies who hang out at the bike rack and hassle the smaller kids. Yeah, you'll even have to learn how to pretend that name-calling doesn't hurt. It'll always hurt, but you'll have to put up a front, or they'll call you worse names next time. I only hope you remember how it feels — in case you ever decide to rank a kid who's smaller than you.

When was the last time I told you I was proud of you? I guess if I can't remember, I've got work to do. I remember the last time I yelled at you — told you we'd be late if you didn't hurry — but, on balance, as Nixon used to say, I haven't given you as many pats as yells. For the record, in case you read this, I am proud of you. I especially like your independence, the way you take care of yourself even when it frightens me just a little bit. You've never been much of a whiner, and that makes you a superior kid in my book.

Why is it that fathers are so slow to realize that eight-year-olds need as many hugs as four-year-olds? If I don't watch out, pretty soon I'll be punching you on the arm and saying, "Whaddaya say, kid?!" instead of hugging you and telling you I love you. Life is too short to hide affection. Why is it that 8-year-olds are so slow to realize that 36-year-olds need as many hugs as 4-year-olds?

Did I forget to tell you that I'm proud you went back to a box lunch after one week's worth of that indigestible hot lunch? I'm glad you value your body.

I wish the drive weren't so short. ... I want to talk about last night ... when your younger brother was asleep and we let you stay up and watch the Yankees game. Those times are so special. There's no way you can plan them. Every time we try to plan something together, it's not as good or rich or warm. For a few all-too-short minutes it was as if you'd already grown up and we sat and talked without any words about "How are you doing in school, son?" I'd already checked your math homework the only way I could — with a calculator. You're better with numbers than I'll ever be. So, we talked about the game, and you knew more about the players than I did, and I learned from you. And we were both happy when the Yankees won.

Well, there's the crossing guard. He'll probably outlive all of us. I wish you didn't have to go to school today. There are so many things I want to say.

Your exit from my car is so quick. I want to savor the moment, and you've already spotted a couple of your friends.

I just wanted to say "I love you, son. ..."

The Perfect American Family

by Michael Murphy

It is 10:30 on a perfect Saturday morning, and we are, for the moment, the perfect American family. My wife has taken our six-year-old to his first piano lesson. Our 14-year-old has not yet roused from his slumber. The four-year-old watches tiny, anthropomorphic beings hurl one another from cliffs in the other room. I sit at the kitchen table, reading the newspaper.

Aaron Malachi, the four-year-old, apparently bored by the cartoon carnage and the considerable personal power obtained by holding the television's remote control, enters my space.

"I'm hungry," he says.

"Want some more cereal?"

"No."

"Want some yogurt?"

"No."

"Want some eggs?"

"No. Can I have some ice cream?"

"No."

For all I know, ice cream may be far more nourishing than processed cereal or antibiotic-laden eggs, but, according to my cultural values, it is wrong to have ice cream at 10:45 on a Saturday morning.

Silence. About four seconds. "Daddy, we have very much of life left, don't we?"

"Yes, we have lots of life left, Aaron."

"Me and you and Mommy?"

"That's right."

"And Isaac?"

"Yes."

"And Ben?"

"Yes. You and me and Mommy and Isaac and Ben."

"We have very much of life left. Until all the people die."

"What do you mean?"

"Until all the people die and the dinosaurs come back."

Aaron sits down on the table, cross-legged like a Buddha, in the center of my newspaper.

"What do you mean, Aaron, 'until all the people die'?"

"You said everybody dies. When everybody dies, then the dinosaurs will come back. The cavemen lived in caves, dinosaur caves. Then the dinosaurs came back and squished 'em."

I realize that already for Aaron life is a limited economy, a resource with a beginning and an end. He envisions himself and us somewhere along that trajectory, a trajectory that ends in uncertainty and loss.

I am faced with an ethical decision. What should I do now? Should I attempt to give him God, salvation, eternity? Should I toss him some spiel like, "Your body is just a shell, and after you die, we will all be together in spirit forever"?

Or should I leave him with his uncertainty and his anxiety because I think it's real? Should I try to make him an anxious existentialist, or should I try to make him feel better?

I don't know. I stare at the newspaper. The Celtics are consistently losing on Friday nights. Larry Bird is angry at somebody, but I can't see who, because Aaron's foot is in the way. I don't know, but my neurotic, addictive, middle-class sensibility is telling me that this is a very important moment, a moment when Aaron's ways of constructing his world are being formed. Or maybe my neurotic, addictive, middle-class sensibility is just making me think that. If life and death are an illusion, then why should I trifle with how someone else understands them?

On the table Aaron plays with an "army guy," raising his arms and balancing him on his shaky legs. It was Kevin McHale that Larry Bird was angry at. No, not Kevin McHale, it was Jerry Sichting. But Jerry Sichting is no longer with the Celtics. Whatever happened to Jerry Sichting? Everything dies, everything comes to an end. Jerry Sichting is playing for Sacramento or Orlando, or he has disappeared.

I should not trifle with how Aaron understands life and death because I want him to have a solid sense of structure, a sense of the permanence of things. It's obvious what a good job the nuns and priests did with me. It was agony or bliss. Heaven and hell were not connected by long-distance service. You were on God's team, or you were in the soup; and the soup was hot. I don't want Aaron to get burned, but I want him to have a strong frame. The neurotic but unavoidable anxiety can come later.

Is that possible? Is it possible to have a sense that God, spirit, karma, Y*H*W*H—something—is transcendent, without traumatizing the presentness of a person, without beating it into them? Can we have our cake and eat it too, ontologically speaking? Or is their fragile sensibility, their "there-ness," sundered by such an act?

Sensing a slight increase in agitation on the table, I know that Aaron is becoming bored with his guy. With an attitude of drama benefiting the moment, I clear my throat and begin with a professional tone.

"Aaron, death is something that some people believe…"

"Dad," Aaron interrupts. "Could we play a video game? It's not a very violent game," he explains, hands gesticulating. "It's not like a killing game. The guys just kind of flop over."

"Yes," I say with some relief, "let's play video games. But first there's something else we have to do."

"What?" Aaron stops and turns from where he has run, already halfway to the arcade.

"First, let's have some ice cream."

Another perfect Saturday for a perfect family. For now.

What's in a Name?

by Hanoch McCarty

I was 11 when Mom remarried. When I was four or five, she and my father had divorced. We'd gone from a bright and cheery ground-floor apartment in a safe, middle-class neighborhood, to a fourth-floor, cramped and darker apartment in a poorer area of New York City. My brother and I often felt lonely and frightened, listening to police and ambulance sirens piercing the night.

In the six years we lived there, I remember envying those friends who had fathers. It was my dream to get a father for myself. My own father had completely left my life — his whereabouts a mystery. I thought that if I had a father, he would be a powerful guardian who would magically defend me against the many perils I felt that I faced in the streets. Somehow, in that childhood fantasy, my new father would not have to work.

He'd just be there for me, whenever I needed him. If other boys menaced me, Super Dad would appear and chase them off. It was pure wish fulfillment, but nonetheless a powerful dream for a frightened little boy.

Suddenly, Frank McCarty appeared in our lives. He was exciting and interesting because he was a New York City police captain of detectives. He had a gold police shield, and there was a gun in a holster on his belt, under his suit coat. I don't remember the day he first appeared, but I do remember the general time and its feeling of excitement and drama. Police were the stuff of movies. Police weren't people you actually knew. I told all my friends about him. Their eyes widened as I described his gun and the stories that he told me about capturing some bad guys.

He didn't like to tell these stories, but my mom wanted him to be accepted by her sons, and she knew what kids liked to hear. She'd cue him to tell a certain story, and he'd acquiesce and patiently tell the story. As he got more deeply into the story, he became animated, and the story took on mythic proportions.

One day, Mom asked me how I would feel if she married Frank. By this time, I was really hooked. He had taken me to the Giants game at the Polo Grounds. He had taken me to Coney Island. He talked with me. He gave me advice on how to fight back when confronted with bullies in the street. His gun gleamed darkly from under his coat. I could have a dad, a protector, someone to take me to the game. "Wow!" I said, "I'd love it!"

The date came. We went to a rural resort hotel whose owner was a friend of my mother's. Another friend of Mom's, a judge, presided over the wedding. I had a dad. Everything was going to be all right now.

I didn't know, as a child of 11, how profoundly my life would change with that one moment.

A bachelor until that point, my new dad had very limited experience with children. He didn't have the opportunity to learn his new parenting job in the natural, step-by-step way that fathers usually do. He never held a baby of his own, shared in the delight of that baby's first steps, or had to take turns feeding that child, dressing him, changing diapers, or any of the countless tasks that parenting means.

He was suddenly thrust into the role of parent, and he retreated to what he knew. His experience with kids had been limited to arresting some. His memories of parenting were of his own father's turn-of-the-century methods. He assumed that he could sit at the head of the table and issue orders that complaisant children would instantly obey.

Unfortunately for him, my mother raised us to be more independent, more participatory in dinner table discussions. We were encouraged to have opinions. She taught us to speak up as well as to listen. We weren't taught to be impolite or rude, but we were contentious.

Complicating all of this was the onset of puberty. Frank McCarty became a father, with his need to be in control, all-knowing, the leader — at the very moment that I was becoming a teen and was in the throes of the adolescent search for independence and self-authority. I was so attracted to him, I almost instantly loved him. Yet, at the same time, I was angry at him almost constantly. He stood in my way. He wasn't easy to manipulate. My brother and I could masterfully manipulate our mother. Frank McCarty was immune to our tricks.

Thus began eight years of pure hell for me and for my new dad. He announced rules, and I tried to flout them. He sent me to my room for rudeness or for my attitude. I complained bitterly to my mother about his dictatorial practices. She tried hard to be the peacemaker but to no avail.

I must admit that there were many occasions in my life from age 13 until I was 20 that I was stuck in a state of anger and frustration at some perceived slight by my father. Passionate as these times were, they were punctuated by great moments with him. Going shopping with him, every week, for flowers to "surprise your mother," he'd say. Going to a ball game. Sitting in a car with him, late at night, watching a house. He'd take me on a surveillance, when he became a private detective back in New York City, if the case was an insurance fraud or something similarly nonviolent. We'd sit there in the darkened car, sipping coffee, and he'd talk about "the job," as he called his career in the police department. I felt so special, so loved, so included at these times. This was exactly what my fantasy had been. A dad who loved me, who'd do things with me.

I remember many, many nights, sitting in front of him on an ottoman, and he'd rub my back as we watched TV together. He gave great hugs. He wasn't afraid to say "I love you." I found the tenderness this rough-and-ready guy was able to express remarkable. However, he could go from these intimate moments to red-faced yelling and sputtering anger if I did or said something that he thought was rude. His temper was a natural phenomenon akin to a tornado. It was a fearsome thing to watch, and it was even scarier to be the target of it.

In high school, the angry moments increased, and my closeness with him decreased. By the time I was in college, I was mostly alienated from him. I got a lot of mileage in terms of sympathy from my friends if I put him down in my conversations with them. I'd tell stories of his latest "atrocity," and stuck in adolescence just as I was, they'd murmur sympathetically about how much we all had to put up with from our dads.

It was my last year in college. I don't know if there was any one event that precipitated it other than my getting a year older and going further along on the road to maturity, but I started rethinking my relationship with him.

I thought, "Here's a guy who falls in love with my mother, and he's stuck with two teenage boys as the price of being married to her. He didn't fall in love with two kids, just my mother. But we came with the package.

"And look what he does: He doesn't just relate to her and ignore us. No, he tries his very hardest to be a real father to me. He risks the relationship all the time. He tried to teach me a set of values. He made me do my homework. He took me to the emergency room at two in the morning. He paid for my education without a grumble. He taught me how to tie a tie. He did all the daddy things without thought of payback. That's really something. I guess I'm a lucky kid to have him in my life."

I knew that my dad had come from an old New England Irish family. They were never famous, powerful or wealthy, but they had been here a long, long time. He felt sad that he was the last to "carry the name." "It'll die with me," he said. His brother had died without children, and his sisters, having married and taken their husbands' names, wouldn't carry on that name either.

My brother and I still carried the name of our biological father, the man who sired me but didn't stay around for the rest of the job. The thought troubled me that the man who really was my father, as I understood that word, would not be celebrated by having a son with his own name.

Ideas occur to us and gradually coalesce into behavior. The idea got stronger and stronger. My thoughts were increasingly taken over by this idea. Finally, action was inevitable. I went to an attorney and then to a court. Secretly, I had my name changed to McCarty. I told no one. I waited three months until my dad's birthday in October.

He opened the birthday card slowly. Usually when I gave him a card, it was attached to a box with his gift. This time there was no box, just the envelope. He pulled out the card and, with it, a certificate from a court.

I wrote on the card, "No store sells true gifts for father and son. You gave me roots, I give you branches."

It was one of only two or three times I ever saw my dad cry. Tears came unbidden to his eyes. He smiled and shook his head and sighed. Then he got up and enfolded me in one of his famous bear hugs. "Thank you, boy, thank you. I just don't know what to say. Thank you." My mom was stunned, too. And very happy for both of us. The war was over. I'd brought the armistice agreement, wrapped in a birthday card.

A Lesson from My Father

by LaVonn Steiner

We come by business naturally in our family. Each of the seven children in our family worked in our father's store, "Our Own Hardware-Furniture Store," in Mott, North Dakota, a small town on the prairies. We started working by doing odd jobs like dusting, arranging shelves and wrapping, and later graduated to serving customers. As we worked and watched, we learned that work was about more than survival and making a sale.

One lesson stands out in my mind. It was shortly before Christmas. I was in the eighth grade and was working evenings, straightening the toy section. A little boy, five or six years old, came in. He was wearing a brown tattered coat with dirty worn cuffs. His hair was straggly, except for a cowlick that stood straight up from the crown of his head. His shoes were scuffed, and his one shoelace was torn. The little boy looked poor to me — too poor to afford to buy anything. He looked around the toy section, picked up this item and that, and carefully put them back in their place.

Dad came down the stairs and walked over to the boy. His steel blue eyes smiled, and the dimple in his cheek stood out as he asked the boy what he could do for him. The boy said he was looking for a Christmas present to buy his brother. I was impressed that Dad treated him with the same respect as any adult. Dad told him to take his time and look around. He did.

After about 20 minutes, the little boy carefully picked up a toy plane, walked up to my dad and said, "How much for this, mister?"

"How much you got?" Dad asked.

The little boy held out his hand and opened it. His hand was creased with wet lines of dirt from clutching his money. In his hand lay two dimes, a nickel and two pennies — 27 cents. The price on the toy plane he'd picked out was $3.98.

"That'll just about do it," Dad said as he closed the sale. Dad's reply still rings in my ears. I thought about what I'd seen as I wrapped the present. When the little boy walked out of the store, I didn't notice the dirty, worn coat, the straggly hair or the single torn shoelace. What I saw was a radiant child with a treasure.

Climbing the Stairway to Heaven

by Joanna Slan

Throughout my career in sales, I've wondered about difficult customers. What makes them so mean? How can they be so unkind? How can a perfectly rational person suddenly lose all sense of human decency?

One day, I had an insight into their thinking. It happened while visiting my husband's music store. He was working with a customer, and we were short-handed. So I did what every good wife would do: I tried to wait on customers.

"I'm looking for music," said a gnarled man, a soiled John Deere cap pulled down tightly over his thinning gray hair. "The name of the song is..." and he uncrumpled a grimy sheet of mimeographed paper from his jeans pocket, "'Stairway to Heaven.' Do you have it?"

I stepped to the wall displays of sheet music and scanned for the name. On a good day, the music filled slots in alphabetical order. On this day, the alphabet skipped around. I searched for several minutes, conscious of his growing restlessness.

"No, I'm sorry, but it doesn't look like it's here."

His back arched, and his watery blue eyes narrowed. Almost imperceptibly, his wife touched his sleeve as if to draw him back. His narrow mouth twisted in anger.

"Well, ain't that just grand. You call yourself a music store? What kind of a store doesn't have music like that? All the kids know that song!" he spluttered.

"Yes, but we don't carry every piece of music ever..."

"Oh, easy for you! Easy to give excuses!" Now his wife was pawing at his sleeve, murmuring, trying to calm him the way a groom talks to a horse gone wild.

He leaned in to me, pointing a knotty finger at my face. "I guess you wouldn't understand, would you? You don't care about my boy dying! About him smashing up his Camaro into that old tree. About them playing his favorite song at his funeral, and he's dead! He's gone! Only 18, and he's gone!"

The paper he waved at me came into focus. It was the program for a memorial service.

"I guess you wouldn't understand," he mumbled. He bent his head. His wife put her arm around him and stood quietly by his side.

"I can't understand your loss," I said quietly, "but we buried my four-year-old nephew last month, and I know how bad that hurts."

He looked up at me. The anger slid from his face, and he sighed. "It's a shame, ain't it? A dirty shame." We stood in silence for a long moment. Then he fished around in his back pocket and pulled out a worn billfold. "Would you like to see a picture of our boy?"

Missed Opportunities

by Nick Lazaris

I had offered to watch my three-year-old daughter, Ramanda, so that my wife could go out with a friend. I was getting some work done while Ramanda appeared to be having a good time in the other room. No problem, I figured. But then it got a little too quiet, and I yelled out, "What are you doing, Ramanda?" No response. I repeated my question and heard her say, "Oh...nothing." *Nothing? What does "nothing" mean?*

I got up from my desk and ran out into the living room, whereupon I saw here take off down the hall. I chased her up the stairs and watched her as her little behind made a hard left into the bedroom. I was gaining on her! She took off for the bathroom. Bad move. I had her cornered. I told her to turn around. She refused. I pulled out my big, mean, authoritative Daddy voice, "Young lady, I said turn around!"

Slowly, she turned toward me. In her hand was what was left of my wife's new lipstick. And every square inch of her face was covered with bright red (except her lips of course)!

As she looked up at me with fearful eyes, lips trembling, I heard every voice that had been shouted to me as a child. "How could you … You should know better than that … How many times have you been told … What a bad thing to do …" It was just a matter of my picking out which old message I was going to use on her so that she would know what a bad girl she had been. But before I could let loose, I looked down at the sweatshirt my wife had put on her only an hour before. In big letters it said, "I'M A PERFECT

LITTLE ANGEL!" I looked back up into her tearful eyes, and, instead of seeing a bad girl who didn't listen, I saw a child of God...a perfect little angel full of worth, value and a wonderful spontaneity that I had come dangerously close to shaming out of her.

"Sweetheart, you look beautiful! Let's take a picture so Mommy can see how special you look." I took the picture and thanked God that I didn't miss the opportunity to reaffirm what a perfect little angel he had given me.

I "Heard" the Love

by Paul Barton

When I was growing up I do not recall hearing the words "I love you" from my father. When your father never says them to you when you are a child, it gets tougher and tougher for him to say those words as he gets older. To tell the truth, I could not honestly remember when I had last said those words to him either. I decided to set my ego aside and make the first move. After some hesitation, in our next phone conversation I blurted out the words, "Dad...I love you!"

There was a silence at the other end, and he awkwardly replied, "Well, same back at ya!"

I chuckled and said, "Dad, I know you love me, and when you are ready, I know you will say what you want to say."

Fifteen minutes later my mother called and nervously asked, "Paul, is everything okay?"

A few weeks later, Dad concluded our phone conversation with the words, "Paul, I love you." I was at work during this conversation, and the tears were rolling down my cheeks as I finally "heard" the love. As we both sat there in tears we realized that this special moment had taken our father/son relationship to a new level.

A short while after this special moment, my father narrowly escaped death following heart surgery. Many times since, I have pondered the thought, *If I did not take the first step and Dad did not survive the surgery, I would have never "heard" the love.*

The Bigger the Better

by Barry Spilchuk

Karen and I were the proud "Parents of the Day" at our son Michael's kindergarten class. We had fun as he toured us around his classroom and introduced us to all his friends. We joined in for cut-and-paste and sewing, and spent the better part of the morning in the sandbox. It was a riot!

"Circle up!" called the teacher. "It's story time." Not wanting to look out of place, Karen and I "circled up" with the rest of our new buddies. After finishing the story, entitled *Big*, the teacher asked this enthusiastic group, "What makes you feel big?"

"Bugs make me feel big," yelled one young student. "Ants," hollered another. "Mosquitoes," called out one more.

The teacher, trying to bring some order back to the class, started calling on children with their hands up. Pointing to one little girl, the teacher said, "Yes, dear, what makes you feel big?" "My mommy," was the reply.

"How does your mommy make you feel big?" quizzed the teacher. "That's easy," said the child. "When she hugs me and says, 'I love you, Jessica!'"

Almie Rose

by Michelle Lawrence

It was at least two months before Christmas when nine-year-old Almie Rose told her father and me that she wanted a new bicycle. As Christmas drew nearer, her desire for a bicycle seemed to fade, or so we thought. We purchased the latest rage, Baby-Sitter's Club dolls, and a dollhouse. Then, much to our surprise, on December 23, she said that she "really wanted a bike more than anything else."

It was just too late, what with all the details of preparing Christmas dinner and buying last-minute gifts, to take the time to select the "right bike" for our little girl. So, here we were — Christmas Eve around 9:00 p.m., with Almie Rose and her six-year-old brother, Dylan, nestled snug in their beds. We could now think only of the bicycle, the guilt and being parents who would disappoint their child.

"What if I make a little bicycle out of clay and write a note that she could trade the clay model in for a real bike?" her dad asked. The theory being that since this is a high-ticket item and she is "such a big girl," it would be much better for her to pick it out. So he spent the next four hours painstakingly working with clay to create a miniature bike.

On Christmas morning, we were excited for Almie Rose to open the little heart-shaped package with the beautiful red and white clay bike and the note. Finally, she opened it and read the note aloud.

"Does this mean that I trade in this bike that Daddy made me for a real one?" Beaming, I said, "Yes."

Almie Rose had tears in her eyes when she replied, "I could never trade in this beautiful bicycle that Daddy made me. I'd rather keep this than get a real bike."

At that moment, we would have moved heaven and earth to buy her every bicycle on the planet!

My Own Experience

by Karrey Janvrin Lindenberg

My first awareness of her was her hands. I don't remember how old I was, but my whole being and existence were associated with those hands. Those hands belonged to my mom, and she is blind.

I can remember sitting at the kitchen table coloring a picture. "Look at my picture, Mom. It's all finished."

"Oh, that's pretty," she replied and kept right on doing whatever she was doing.

"No, look at my picture with your fingers," I insisted. She then came to me, and I ran her hand all over the picture. I always enjoyed her excited response that the picture was lovely.

It never occurred to me that it was strange how she felt things with her hands, how she touched my face or things I showed her. I did realize that my dad looked at me and at the things I showed to him with his eyes, and so did Grandma or any other person who came into our house; but I never thought it unusual that Mom didn't use her eyes.

I can still remember how she combed my long hair. She put the thumb of her left hand between my eyebrows, just at the top of my nose, and her forefinger at the crown of my head. She was probably lining up those two points, and then she'd bring the comb from her forefinger down to meet the thumb. Thus, she hoped the part would be down the middle of my head. I never questioned her ability to do this task.

When I fell down many times at play, came in crying and told Mom that my knee was bleeding, her gentle hands washed my knee and skillfully applied a bandage.

One day I found out, unfortunately, that there were certain things my mother wouldn't touch. I found a tiny dead bird lying on the sidewalk in front of our house and brought it into the house to show Mom. "Look what I found," I said as I took her hand to touch the bird. "What is it?" she asked. She lightly touched the dead creature in my outstretched palm, and I could hear the terror in her voice as she asked once more, "What is it?"

"A little dead bird," I answered. She screamed then quickly drew back her hand, ordered me and the bird outside, and admonished me never to let her touch such a thing again.

I could never quite reckon with her powers of smell, hearing and touch. One day, I saw a plate of cookies that Mom had just placed on the table. I slyly took one and looked at her to see what she would say. She didn't say a word, and, of course, I thought as long as she didn't feel with those hands what I'd done, she didn't know. I didn't realize that she could hear me chew. Just as I passed by her, munching my cookie, she caught my arm. "Next time, Karrey, please ask me for that cookie instead of taking it," she said. "You can have all you want, just ask next time."

I have an older brother and sister and a younger brother, and none of us could quite figure out how she knew which one of us did a certain thing. One day my older brother brought a stray dog into the house and sneaked him up the stairs into his bedroom. In a short while my mom marched up the stairs, opened his bedroom door and ordered the dog to be put outside. We were amazed she figured out there was a dog in the house.

As I grew older, I realized that Mom reared us psychologically. And with those sharp ears and nose of hers, she put two and two together and usually came up with the right answer. She had heard the dog's toenails clicking on the bedroom floor.

And that nose of hers. How it knew so much! One day my friend and I were playing with dolls in my bedroom. I slipped into Mom's room and doused the dolls with some of her perfume. Then I made the mistake of running downstairs to ask Mom a question. She immediately told me that she knew I had been in her bedroom and used her perfume.

Those ears. How they knew the things we did. I was all alone in the living room one night, doing my homework with the TV running softly. Mom walked into the room and asked, "Karrey, are you doing your homework or watching TV?" I was slightly surprised but answered her and went on with my homework. Later I thought about it and wondered how she knew that I was the one in the living room and not one of my brothers or my sister. I asked her. "Sorry, honey," she said, patting my head. "Even though your adenoids are gone, you still breathe through your mouth. I heard you."

Mom had a good sense of direction, too. She had a tandem bicycle, and we took turns riding with her. I sat on the front seat and steered and pedaled, and she sat on the back seat. She always seemed to know where we were and called out directions loud and clear. She always knew when we were approaching an intersection or when a fast-moving car was coming up on the right side.

How did she know that while I was taking a bath one night, when I was about nine years old, I hadn't washed any part of myself? I was busy playing with the toys in the water and having a great time. "Karrey, you haven't touched your face or ears or anything, have you?" I hadn't, but how did she know? Of course she knew that a little girl playing with toys in a bathtub would not stop to wash. I realized that she also used her mind's eye in rearing us.

The one thing, however, that used to concern us was the fact that Mom never really knew what we looked like. One day when I was about 17 and standing in front of the bathroom mirror combing my hair, I asked, "You really don't know what any of us look like, do you, Mom?" She was feeling my hair to see how long it was.

"Of course I do," she answered.

"I know what you looked like the day they laid your tiny little body in my arms for the first time. I felt every inch of you and felt the soft fuzz on your head. I knew that you were blond because your daddy told me so. I knew that your eyes were blue because they told me so. I know that you are very pretty because people tell me you are. But I really know what you are like — what you are like inside." My eyes grew misty.

"I know that you're lithe and strong because you love being on the tennis court. I know that you have a good nature because I hear you talk to the cat and to small children. I know you are tenderhearted. I know you are vulnerable because I've seen your hurt reactions to someone's remarks. I know that you have character because you have the courage to stand up and defend your convictions. I know that you have a respect for human beings because of the way you treat me. I know that you have wisdom because you conduct yourself wisely for a girl your age. I also know that you have a will of your own because I've seen a hint of temper, which tells me that no one can dissuade you from doing the right things. I know that you have family devotion because I've heard you defending your brothers and sister. I know that you possess a great capacity for love because you've shown it to me and to your father many times. You have never indicated in any way that you were short-changed because you have a blind mother. So, dear," and she drew me close to her, "I see you, and I know exactly what you look like, and to me you are beautiful."

That was 10 years ago, and recently I became a mother. When they laid my precious little son in my arms, I, like my mother, was able to see my child and know how beautiful he was. The only difference was that I could see him with my eyes. But sometime I'd like to turn out the lights, hold and touch him, and see if I can feel all the things my mother felt.